About this Book

This book is not a comprehensive book. Rather, this book is designed to spark creative thinking regarding how a parent or caregiver can use money to begin their children's financial future, giving them the financial boost they need in life.

I cover topics and give examples and options that may give the foundation needed to benefit the future of any child. I help you to rethink the idea of pocket change, while writing this book, I assumed that you are looking for a way to secure a financial future for your baby.

Look no further, this book is the building block to a new generation of future financial thinkers!

I0477968

Dedication

I dedicate this book to my beautiful baby girl, Kalyn. Kalyn is my precious treasure, I love you baby girl. I thank God for you every day.

Broke Millionaire Baby

What do you want to be when you grow up? Isn't that a loaded question and frankly a lot of pressure. Some start asking this question as soon as their baby goes to kindergarten. Instead of asking, what are you going to do or where are you going to work when you grow up?

How about asking, how much money do you think you want to make or how much of your time do you want to trade for money? Maybe we should ask ourselves these questions.

Babies grow up thinking they are supposed to become something. How about they be themselves and have a profession. Stop the madness and embrace a new question. The question every one of their friends will be asking; How are you a millionaire at 40 years old? The answer, compound interest, mom/dad invested in my financial future from birth.

Broke Millionaire Baby is about changing your baby's financial future by changing your spending habits and investing as they grow into an adult.

Secure your baby's financial future!

BABY, BABY, BABY ...

The news of a baby is such a wonderful, blissful, and happy event. In fact, we run to the nearest baby store ready to buy tiny precious "baby must haves" and the shopping begins. Stop, put the baby clothes down! Without thinking we spend our babies' future.

Before our babies first breath we purchase an entire array of baby treasures and why not, buying baby clothes is so exciting. No, it's stupid, but we can't help ourselves everything is so CUTE. I'm not saying don't buy any baby clothes. I am saying don't buy a lot of baby clothes.

Sometimes we start buying baby "stuff" before we know if we are having a girl or boy. The excitement is too great besides that's what we are supposed to do, right? Wrong, that's the norm. The next thing we know the house is full of new baby clothes, furniture, strollers, and toys; It's baby shopping madness! Let's not forget about the "baby shower". It's not enough that we impulse to buy every baby thing we see, but we must get everyone else to buy baby too.

Stop, the madness!

Step 1

Stop the Madness

Why do we spend hundreds or worse thousands of dollars on baby "stuff" that we will soon give away, sell at the fraction of the cost, pack up and hoard for keepsake or simply throw away?

Simple, we are conditioned to think we need to set our new babies up with 50 new outfits, 10 pair of shoes, 15 blankets, a memory foam mattress, and create an entire room painted especially in baby appropriate colors, diapers, wipes, lotions, and special crib lights for a night light that they will most likely never remember. Okay, they will if you keep everything the same for the first four to five years. Who are we kidding all the stuff is not for the baby, it's for us. Stop, the madness.

The madness is robbing their financial future!

Fast forward, birthday number one, complete madness! Everything must be number one specific, the cake, banner, candle, gifts, outfit, and invitations for a blessed price upward of $200, but why? Who are we kidding the parties are for us. The baby will not remember the first four or think about them until we show them photo's or show the photos to their first "love". Personally, the latter is more fun.

However, we don't stop there we continue the madness through every birthday and a soon as possible we start with holiday spending madness. Eventually, we spend thousands on parties, gifts, and holiday's. Stop, the madness!

The average cost for one birthday party is $200, if you spend less, great! Keep in mind, the older they get the more we spend.

$200 X 18 = $3,600

Holidays are a different ball game, we spend hundreds to thousands on one holiday for one baby and why? We are conditioned to think we should and in turn they begin to expect it; conditioning them that they deserve a $400 video gaming system.

Stop, the average cost for one special spectacular Christmas morning is $400. (maybe more or less).

$400 per Christmas X 18 Christmases = $7,200

Realize we spend an average of $10,800 in parties and gifts for two events a year for 18 years. Of course, some will spend more, and some will spend less. Hang on and think, $10,800 will cover one year of tuition at a community college, put a down payment on a first house, or buy a respectable first car.

$3,600 + $7,200 = $10,800

I am not saying don't buy your baby gifts or have a birthday party for 18 years. I am saying, watch your dollars. How, many of us have all our gifts from our first to 18th birthday or Holiday? Do you think your soon to be adult will? Of course not.

STOP the madness and spend a small amount and invest the rest in their future! They are going to be asking you for money at one time or another, might as well plan for it.

Is your baby going to remember the 100 teddy bears you bought them or the $100,00 (maybe) you had waiting for them at age 18 to go to college, buy a house, new car, or reinvest for their millionaire retirement. Yes, it is possible to have $100,000 waiting for them to graduate high school, if you plan and invest.

Many seem to be shocked that they can't afford to send their baby to college after high school because they can't afford the tuition, as if it was a shock or surprise that 18 years later they might go to college. If I have a baby and it grows to graduate high school, do you need money for college? Uh, YES!

Stop the madness!

Set a standard and invest in your baby's million-dollar future. They could be a 40-year-old millionaire just off mommy and daddy investing in their future. Even better question, who of us wouldn't love to thank our parents for making us a millionaire while we grew up with a few less gifts.

Baby's got More Money!

BROKE MILLIONAIRE BABY MONEY

Secure your baby's financial future!

Step 2

Don't listen to the Norm

The norm is wrong! We all have that friend or family member or both that thinks you must go all out for every birthday and every holiday.

Don't listen to them, their baby will be asking your baby how they have a million dollars at 40 years old, especially when they didn't have to make it themselves. How can they buy a new house, car, and boat, for his or her wife or start their baby's millionaire future?

Your special baby is worth more than throwing your money away on the next big trend or what friends and family tell you to do with your money. Let your friends and family spend their money on whatever they want for their baby but, you must think and invest in your baby's future. People will tell you you're being greedy, stingy, and mean for not buying your child a new $600 cell phone every year.

Don't listen your baby has a millionaire future because his/her parents thought their financial future was more important than the next laptop, cellphone, or cool pair of jeans. Not that there is anything wrong with those things they just aren't necessary for a small child or teenager.

It's okay to have a million-dollar secret stash waiting. There will be times your baby is upset that they don't have the "cool" stuff that all the other kids have and that is okay. Your baby may not know they have a stash of cash waiting for them to grow up, but they will love you to the moon and back when they find out! Nothing says I love you more than sacrificing a few right-now's for a multi-million-dollar retirement.

Imagine your Baby's Financial Future

Invest in their Future!

Step 3

Grandma's "Rainy Day"

Turns out grandma was one smart lady! Grandma always said, "you have to save for a rainy day" and it turns out she was right.

However, most put the "rainy day" on a credit card. But, what if you didn't? Grandma and Grandpa thought a quarter was a lot of money. Turns out a quarter can be a lot of money if you put it with more quarters. Four quarters equal one dollar, but one dollar turns into two and two dollars into three.

How do you turn one dollar into three dollars? Easy, add more quarters! Sounds simple, right? It is a lot simpler to put a quarter away for a rainy day than a dollar. Pocket change goes a long way when you invest it in a college fund for 18 years; without compound interest a single $4.78 coffee purchase a week over 18 years gives your baby $205.92, good "rainy day" fund, just like grandma said.

$5.00 - $4.78 = 0.22 (less than a quarter)

52 wks. X 18 yrs. = 936

0.22 X 936 = $205.9

Step 4

Half the Gift Money

Grandma's gift giving every birthday and holiday may be worth more than you ever imagined. What if grandma took half the gift money and put it in your baby's college fund, IRA, or savings account? Grandma's $50 gift may turn into a $25 gift, but $25 a year for 18 years is $450. The "rainy day" now has $605.92 stashed away.

$25 X 18 = $450

$450 + $205.92 = $605.92

Maybe another family member or friend blesses your baby by stashing cash for their future. Half the Holiday gifts, instead of Grandma, Aunt, and Uncle spending $100 on a gift they spend $50 and put the other $50 in your baby's college fund, IRA, or savings for 18 years. Let's do the math.

Grandma $50 + Aunt $50 + Uncle $50 = $150

$150 X 18 = $2,700

$2,700 + $605.92 = $3,305.92

Wow, what 18-year-old needs $3,305.92? A broke 18-year-old baby, your baby! Most adults today don't have $1000 in a savings account.

What could be better than having $3,306.92 at 18 years-old? How about adding a clothing allowance each year and slashing 10% off and stashing it away? Most of us spend at least $500 every August going store to store purchasing "back-to-school" clothes. Your 18-year-old baby has $4,205.92!

10% of $500 = $50

$50 X 18 years = $900

$900 + $3,305.92 = $4205.

Do the ....

Step 5

Baby's stash of cash

Okay, now you're listening, and you want to know where the millions are. We will get to that, but first, where do you stash the cash? There are many ways to start your baby out on the right financial track and some are better than others.

- A savings account is good, but it usually only has a 1% return. Meaning, it would require a substantial amount to reflect any kind of increase.

- A college fund is better than a savings account in two ways. One, with a savings account you may be tempted to use the money when you have a "rainy day" (bad idea). A college fund maybe set up through an employer or a brokerage. Opening a college fund is easy, simply find a broker or sign up through your employer and have a set amount taken directly from your paycheck.

- An Individual Retirement Account or IRA (traditional or Roth) is like a 401K. An IRA permits you to invest money in stocks or mutual funds which accumulates compound interest for retirement. A traditional IRA is a retirement plan that enables the investor (you) to invest in stocks or mutual fund(s) earning compound interest over a period and you pay taxes when you retire. A Roth IRA is a retirement account that enables the investor (you) to invest in stocks or mutual fund(s) earning compound interest over a period and taxes are paid at the time of investment.

There are a couple of options when opening an IRA. Use a financial broker and open an account investing a planned dollar amount and identify your baby as the accounts beneficiary(s) or consult a broker enabling you to set an IRA that may transfer funds to another retirement account started when your baby starts their own IRA. Consult a financial advisor or broker before opening an IRA.

Example:

I opened a Roth IRA (separate from my own) and I make regular cash deposits with my daughter as the beneficiary. In addition, I had my daughter open her Roth IRA online when she turned 22 and I write a check to deposit funds into her account investing in her retirement while she makes regular deposits herself investing more into her financial future.

Step 6

Growing money as your baby grows

First and foremost, we all know it doesn't matter how old our baby maybe they are still our baby. Therefore, you must put money away for your baby's future. I have given everyday examples of the easiest ways to stash your baby cash by using money you already obtain or spend.

How does money grow? Answer, compound interest. What is compound interest? Did you know money can work while you sleep? Compound interest is your money working for you. How does your money work for you? When you invest, your money makes money for you by the way of compound interest.

Example 1:

You invest $1000 on a stock or mutual fund that returns 10% in one year.

$1000 X 10% = $100

$1000 + $100 = $1100 (year one you have $1100)

The next year the stock or mutual fund returns 10% again.

$1100 X 10% = $110

$110 + $1100 = $1210 (year two you have $1210)

Your initial $1000 is now $1210 and you did <u>nothing</u>.

Compound interest is interest that builds upon on the principle amount and the interest accumulated! This continues and the more money you invest the more principle and interest you have. The trick is to start early (at birth)!

Example 2:

You invest the coffee, birthday, and Christmas money.

$0.25 (quarter a week) X 52 weeks = $13.00 + $150 (half gift money) + $100 (birthday money) = $263

$263 invested in a stock or mutual fund for one year that receives 10% return.

Year 1   **$263 X 10% = $26.30**

            $263 + 26.30 = $289.30

Your baby now has $289.30

Year 2   **$289.30 (year 1 money) + $263 (year 2 investment) = $552.30**

            $552.30 X 10% =$55.23

            $55.23 + $552.30 = $607.53

Your baby now has $607.53

Are you starting to see how it works? Let's get real with the math. You invest $21.63 ($263 / 12) a month in an IRA with a mutual fund or stock averaging 10% a year for 18 years.

Approximately how much money will you have waiting for your baby in 18 years, $11,995.98. At age 25 your baby starts adding $100 a month into their IRA until they retire at age 65. Approximately, how much money do they have in their IRA, **$6,026,293.66**. Your baby is a multi-millionaire.

Baby's got a big stash of cash

What's in your account?

My broke baby is a millionaire

Although, your baby maybe broke in the sense that he/she does not have the money available to them until they turn a certain age, go to college or retire. What you have given them is the boost they need to succeed financially. The financial freedom to live their life and enjoy their family and you did it a little at a time, day-after-day, year-after-year, relieving years of financial pain from yourself and them.

What happens when you retire, and your baby has more in their IRA than you do? Enjoy life and take pride in putting your baby in the top 1% of the population.

Final Broke Millionaire Baby Bonus!

If you want to ensure your baby understands they will be a millionaire and how important it is to maintain their financial future, let them in on the plan. Once a baby gets to a certain (age may differ) teach them how to invest money. Show them and allow them to half their gift money, subtract the 10% clothing allowance, and save the coffee change and then show them how to invest it or save it by assisting them in the process.

Teach and give them a life lesson in personal finance. Keep in mind you can ensure your babies financial future regardless how much money you make if you invest some in their future from birth. Of course, the amount invested will directly affect the return. Moreover, more is better, but do what you can.

Don't be the norm. Stop, the madness!

Your new financial language

You do not have to be rich to become rich!

You may not be rich, but your baby can be rich.

Invest your coffee change.

Invest half of the amount of every gift.

Invest half of the amount of every party.

If your child is born you need money for college.

You can afford to invest at least $20 a month on your baby's future.

A traditional 401K retirement plan is a retirement plan through an employer and is tax differed.

A traditional IRA is set up through a financial broker and is tax differed.

A ROTH IRA is set up through a financial broker and is taxable.

A college fund is set up through a financial broker or an employer.

ROI is the return on an investment.

Compound interest is the accumulated interest on the principal amount invested and the previous interest.

From the Author

Invest time in learning how to make your money work for you and consult a financial broker before investing on your own. Invest in stocks or mutual funds that have a five to 10-year history of at least an average 10% annual yield.

Don't be afraid of the market, there will be highs and lows, the trick is to be in it for the long haul. Remember, stop the madness and don't throw your babies financial future away on "stuff"!

- *Chas H. Howieson, MPH*

Broke Millionaire Baby

Notes: